JUN - 2010

W9-DDJ-038

3 1524 00544 9501

TANKS

WITHDRAWN

Woodridge Public Library

GEOFF CORNISH

Lerner Publications Company
Minneapolis

WOODRIDGE PUBLIC LIBRARY
3 PLAZA DRIVE
WOODRIDGE, IL 60517-5014
(630) 964-7899

First American edition published by Lerner Publications Company.

Copyright © 2003 by The Brown Reference Group plc.

All U.S. rights reserved. No part of this book may be reproduced, stored in a retrieval system, or by any means—electronic or mechanical, photocopying, recording, or otherwise—without permission in writing from Lerner Publications Company, except for the inclusion of brief quotations in an acknowledged review.

Lerner Publications Company.
A division of Lerner Publishing Group
241 First Avenue North
Minneapolis, MN 55401 U.S.A

Website address: www.lernerbooks.com

Library of Congress Cataloging-in-Publication Data

Cornish, Geoff.
 Tanks / by Geoff Cornish.
     p. cm.—(Military hardware in action)
Includes index.
Summary: Profiles some of the different tanks and other armored
fighting vehicles used by armies around the world, describing their
design, weapons, and uses.
 ISBN 0–8225–4701–5 (lib. bdg.)
1. Tanks (Military science)—Juvenile literature. 2. Armored vehicles,
3. Military—Juvenile literature. [1. Tanks (Military science) 2. Armored
Vehicles, Military.] I. Title. II Series.
 UG446.5 .C63 2003
 623.7'4752—dc21   2002009443

Printed in China
Bound in the United States of America
1 2 3 4 5 6 – OS – 08 07 06 05 04 03

This book uses black and yellow chevrons as a decorative element on some headers. They do not point to other elements on the page.

Contents

Introduction

Hull down, motor throbbing, a squat metal hulk lies in a dip at the edge of a wood. Suddenly, there is a blinding flash. It is followed an instant later by an ear-crunching crash from the cannon.

On the horizon, a building or enemy tank disappears in a burst of flame. The tank quietly slips out of sight. The tank is perhaps the most-feared weapon in ground warfare.

World War I

Tanks first appeared during World War I (1914–1918). Commanders needed to get attacking forces across the muddy, open terrain of **no-man's-land** without getting cut down by machine-gun fire. Armored vehicles with wheels could not cross the churned-up ground. By adding **caterpillar tracks**, a main gun, and gun ports (openings) to the sides, the tank was born.

THE FIRST TANKS

A tank on a bank advertisement. Engineers developed tanks during World War I. They used "tank" as a code name. Officially, the vehicles were "self-propelled bullet-proof land-ships," but the simpler name stuck.

WHAT ARE AFVs?

An armored fighting vehicle (AFV) is any military machine that is equipped with defensive armor and offensive weapons and that is able to move using its own motor. AFVs include tanks of all kinds, armored personnel carriers (APCs), self-propelled guns (SPGs), and armored cars (often called armored reconnaissance vehicles or ARVs). APCs and ARVs usually have wheels in place of tracks. The king of AFVs is the tank. It combines striking power, speed, and a defensive layer of armor plate. The main battle tank (MBT) is the largest and hardest hitting of them all.

World War II

AFVs led the German blitzkrieg (lightning war) in Europe at the start of World War II (1939–1945). Tanks, armored cars, and even motorcycles raced through enemy positions. Supported by bombers, AFVs created surprise and confusion with the speed of their attack. Soldiers, cannons, and guns followed behind, to mop up any remaining opposition.

SHERMANS VS GERMANS

A U.S. M4 Sherman comes ashore after the June 1944 **D day** landings.

>> **D day** – Allied invasion of German-occupied Normandy, June 6, 1944

SPEED AND MOBILITY

The German Army swept through Europe quickly due to the mobility and firepower of its tanks. Most of these tanks were small but had speed and ease of movement. The first big tank-on-tank battles occurred later in World War II, at El Alamein in North Africa, at Kursk in Russia, and in France after D day.

RIDING HIGH

The PzKfw (**Panzer**) IV was Germany's frontline assault tank of the 1939 and 1940 blitzkrieg.

DESERT WARFARE

Deserts make ideal tank battlegrounds. A series of tank battles was fought across the Western Desert of Libya and Egypt between 1941 and 1944. Allied forces finally drove the elite German desert troops, known as the Afrika Korps, out of North Africa. Germany abandoned its attempt to reach the Middle East oil fields.

NORTH AFRICAN CAMPAIGN

Afrika Korps Panzer IV tanks in World War II

Cold War Years

After World War II ended in 1945, Europe became divided into two areas of influence. Western European democracies, supported by the United States, faced the Communist countries of Eastern Europe, dominated by the Soviet Union. Both sides combined their forces, creating the North Atlantic Treaty Organization (NATO) in the West and the Warsaw Pact in the East. This 45-year period of armed peace was called the Cold War.

ARMORED TRUST

Both sides expected that a **conventional** war in Europe would begin with an armored blitzkrieg-style attack. During this time, NATO and the Warsaw Pact forces concentrated on developing faster and bigger armored fighting vehicles.

ATTACK

Soviet forces move westward in a **simulated** World War III exercise in the 1980s. Soviet armor was less advanced than its Western opponents. But the Soviets had almost twice as many tanks. Communist leaders hoped to succeed by the sheer weight of their numbers.

COUNTER ATTACK

NATO armored forces based in Germany meet imaginary Warsaw Pact invaders during a simulated exercise in 1984.

09FD10

>> **conventional** – nonnuclear combat, using soldiers and cannons

After the Wall

In the 1990s, the collapse of Communist governments in the Soviet Union and Eastern Europe changed the shape of future combat. Leaders no longer expected tank battles in Europe. Instead, attention shifted to regional flashpoints like Iraq, Bosnia, the Middle East, and Afghanistan.

FAST REACTION

An M551 Sheridan light tank waits to board a C-130 Hercules transport aircraft bound for Saudi Arabia in 1991. Local wars and peacekeeping missions demand lightweight, air-mobile AFVs rather than the heavy MBTs developed during World War II and the Cold War.

The Tank's Job

The main role of the tank is to provide cover for advancing ground forces. Tanks take out enemy defenses and clear the way for infantry following behind. Tanks are good **deterrents**, particularly against small groups of lightly armed soldiers. Some AFVs are **amphibious** and can "swim" across rivers. They have motors that can drive propellers as well as tracks or wheels.

ARMORED TRUST

The new U.S. advanced amphibious assault vehicle (AAAV) can carry up to 18 marines. It has a top speed of 29 mph in the water and 45 mph on land. Power is switched between high-speed water jets and the main tracks. The AAAV has a 30mm main gun, with a 7.62mm machine gun support weapon.

Bridge laying, mine clearing, towing, and trench digging are just some of the many jobs a modern tank can perform.

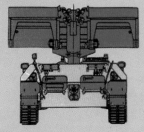

☐ Bridge-laying equipment

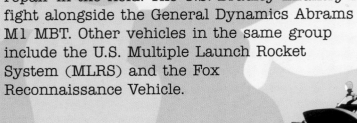

AFV Families

Many modern fighting vehicles are designed to work with other vehicles. Sometimes they are developed by several companies or even by two or more friendly nations. This makes them cheaper to build but also easier to repair in the field. The U.S. Bradley infantry fighting vehicle was built to fight alongside the General Dynamics Abrams M1 MBT. Other vehicles in the same group include the U.S. Multiple Launch Rocket System (MLRS) and the Fox Reconnaissance Vehicle.

BRADLEY FAMILY

The Bradley M2 infantry fighting vehicle carries up to seven fully equipped soldiers to the battlefront. Its protective armor and powerful main gun put down enemy fire.

amphibious

Tank Sizes

There are three main categories of tank: light, medium, and heavy. Light tanks are quick and easy to move and can be **airlifted.**

Light and Medium Tanks

QUICK STINGER

Stingray light tanks. The Stingray was developed in the United States as a replacement for the M551 Sheridan, which was retired from active service.

ALL-AROUNDER

A U.S Army M48 Medium Tank. It has four crewmembers and an M41 90mm main gun. The M48 is a lighter version of the M60 MBT. Medium tanks are general-purpose vehicles. They are light enough for easy transport but still pack a punch.

Heavy Tank

The heavy tank, or main battle tank (MBT), is the big-hitter. It is most effective in tank-on-tank combat, where the most powerful or best armored tank usually wins.

BIG CAT POWER

Germany's Leopard 2 was developed alongside the Abrams M1. It also has a crew of four and a 120mm M256 **smoothbore cannon**.

DETAILS

Main Gun
L55 120mm cannon

Range
545 yards

Fire Control
Heat-seeking sight
Laser targeting

The Tank's Crew

Most tanks have a crew of three or four. These are usually the commander, the driver, the gunner, and sometimes the loader. Vehicles adapted with special equipment, like anti-aircraft (AA) missiles or bridge-laying gear, sometimes carry crewmembers with skills in these tasks. APCs like the Bradley also have room to carry extra troops.

Inside the Abrams

THE CREW

The Abrams has four crewmembers. The commander **(a)** sits in the top of the **turret** with radio contact to the command tank leader and is in charge of the mission. The gunner **(b)** also sits in the turret, at right. The gunner identifies and **ranges** the target, firing the main gun when the commander gives the order. The gunner also operates the roof-hatch machine gun. The loader **(c)** supplies the gunner with the correct ammunition. The loader sits on the left of the turret. The driver **(d)** sits in the hull (main body) steering the tank. The commander and the driver can both control the tank.

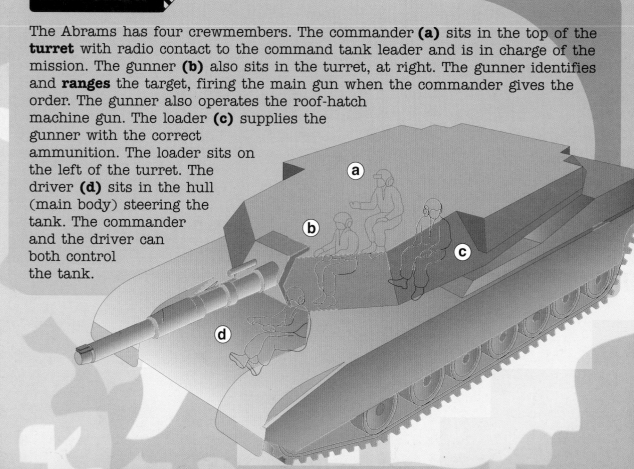

DRIVING THE M1 ABRAMS

"The Abrams is a delight to drive, and makes for a very stable firing platform."

Master Sergeant Frank Wess
Persian Gulf, 1991

TANK TRAINING

After nine weeks of initial combat training, armored unit recruits learn AFV mechanics and tactics at the U.S. Army Armor Center in Fort Knox, Kentucky. Tactical training combines computer-generated experience with actual ground exercises. This is where the tank crew learns its job. They cover subjects such as driving over different kinds of ground and keeping out of sight. Other topics include target ranging and cooperation with other forces.

SUFFIELD

Allied armored units gather for exercises at NATO's international tank training ground at Suffield, Alberta, Canada.

Learning the Trade

A building at the U.S. Army Armor Center is called "the Cave." It contains rows of AFV **simulators**. Here, trainees can experience any of the situations they may face in combat. Instructors can monitor them in a safe environment.

LIVE FIRING

An Abrams M1A1 fires a live round at the Fort Knox Armor Center range during training.

LYING LOW

A gunner practices range finding in an Abrams M1 tank simulator at the Armor Center.

>> **simulator** – computerized training machine that can fake battle conditions

NIGHT FIGHTING

Live night-firing exercises train crews to identify and hit targets in darkness. **Infrared** sights light the target, and laser markers lock on to it. Only the commander and gunner can see the whole picture. They must give accurate instructions to the driver and loader. Night fighting has only been made possible by infrared technology. In World War II, tank battles used to stop during hours of darkness.

BLINDING FLASH

Gunners and drivers stay out of sight, hatches closed, when firing at night. The bright flash during firing can temporarily blind the eyes. Commanders watch for a successful hit.

>> **infrared** – invisible light rays produced by heat that can be detected

Modern AFV Weapons

AFVs have many different types of weapons. These include smoothbore and **rifled cannons**, machine guns, rockets, and anti-aircraft missiles.

CHAPARRAL

Above: An M730 Chaparral guided missile carrier

MAIN GUN

The most important part of a tank is usually the gun mounted in the turret. The M1 Abrams has an M256 120mm smoothbore cannon, built jointly by Germany and the United States. The cannon is also fitted to Germany's Leopard 2 main battle tank. It can fire a variety of weapons, from high explosive to armor piercing. The turret can rotate, and the gun can be raised or lowered. It can be aimed independently of the direction of the tank itself. It can attack or defend itself from all directions.

ABRAMS M1 MBT

ARMAMENT

Main Armament
M256 120mm cannon

Secondary Armament
M240 2 x 7.62mm machine guns

Additional Armament
0.5 in Browning machine gun
on AA mount

ARMOR

The exact makeup of the Abrams's armor is
top secret. It is made from **laminated** plastic.
This makes it very strong. It covers the top,
sides, and front of the tank, protecting it from
all but a rear attack. Plastic, nylon, and
ceramic materials are replacing conventional
steel armor on many modern AFVs.

Bradley Bushmaster

The newest Bradley M3 cavalry fighting vehicle has a 35/50mm Bushmaster **chain gun.** It can carry up to 900 rounds of ammunition on board. The standard Bradley M2 gun is a smaller M242 25mm automatic gun.

TOW POWER

The Bradley can also fire TOW 2 anti-tank missiles.

THE MLRS

The MLRS is designed to work alongside the Abrams tank and the Bradley infantry or cavalry fighting vehicles. It can fire a barrage of small rockets or a large single missile.

Self-Defense

SMOKESCREEN

Most AFVs need weapons of defense. Smoke bombs throw up a curtain of smoke to hide the vehicle while it gets ready for action.

STEEL RAIN

The MLRS earned its nickname, "Steel Rain," during Operation Desert Storm against Iraq in 1991. It is built using the same **chassis** as the M2/M3 and is part of the Bradley family of AFVs.

Famous Tank Battles

Tanks are **tactical weapons**. They win battles, not wars. But some of history's major tank battles have had a lot to do with the later outcome of the war.

World War I

During November 1917, 300 British tanks pushed four miles deep into enemy territory at Cambrai, France. By World War I standards, this was a remarkable feat. Most infantry attacks had gotten no farther than a few hundred yards at best. Tanks had been tried earlier but without much success. They became stuck in the soft mud. At Cambrai, however, the ground was dry, so the tanks moved forward rapidly. It was a turning point in armored warfare.

CAMBRAI

British tanks rolled over the dry ground at Cambrai without getting stuck.

AMERICANS AT THE ARGONNE

U.S. tanks during the **Argonne** offensive in 1918. The force of so much firepower and fresh combatants from the United States convinced Germany to start cease-fire negotiations.

World War II

▶ The world's biggest tank battle was fought at Kursk, in Russia. Operation Citadel was the last all-out German offensive of World War II. In July 1943, German leader Adolf Hitler hurled 1,800 tanks against a massive Soviet force of 3,600 tanks and armor.

NAZI DEFEAT

Soviet troops pass a burning German tank during the Battle of Kursk. German armor failed to break through the Soviet defense. After 10 days of intense combat, the Russians halted the German attack.

Hitler Halted

Having taken over most of western Europe, Hitler invaded the Soviet Union, especially Russia in 1941. German forces swiftly overran much of western Russia. The coming of winter and the fierce fight put up by Soviet troops and tanks stopped the German advance.

LEGENDARY SOVIET T34

Many people say that the Soviet T34 tank was the most outstanding tank of World War II. The T34 borrowed an American design. **Artillery shells** bounced off its two-inch thick sloping armor, and it had a powerful 76.2mm or 85mm main gun. It was tougher than many other tanks, because it was built to cope with harsh Russian winters. Its diesel engine also did not catch fire easily.

LUXURIOUS

"The T34 was fast, and powerful. We felt safe inside."

Nicolai Dubrovin, T34 tank commander, Russian front 1942

>> **artillery shell** = the explosive cartridge of a large gun

Battle for Normandy

Allied forces landed on the beaches of Normandy, France, on D day. At first, the Germans held back their tanks. They thought the main invasion was coming farther north, at Calais. However, after aides convinced Hitler the invasion had started for real, he ordered some of his toughest Panzer **divisions** into action.

TIGER POWER

A King Tiger in France. Germany's Tiger tank was probably the most-feared armored vehicle in World War II.

MICHAEL WITTMAN

Germany's top-scoring tank ace was Michael Wittman (*center, hands on hips, with his Tiger tank crew in Normandy*). He was killed during the fighting.

War-winning Sherman

The most-famous Allied tank of World War II was the M4 Sherman. Some 48,000 M4 Sherman tanks were built during the war, more than double the total number of tanks produced by Germany. Although it was no match for Germany's 60-ton Tiger tank in firepower or armor, the Shermans overwhelmed the enemy with sheer numbers.

MASS PRODUCTION

During the war, 10,000 men and women worked three shifts per day, 6 days a week, in 11 tank factories across the United States. Each Sherman comprised 4,537 parts. It had a 75mm main gun and weighed 33 tons. The M4 also had .30 and .50 **caliber** machine guns.

"I just loved it—the Sherman tank was a 33-ton monster."

John Semmes,
Sherman tank commander, World War II

f an inch

"If you got hit, you were in really good shape to go up just like a match … you had to get out of there as quickly as possible."

Martin Goldstein, M4 driver

WEAK POINT ▷

The Germans called M4s "Ronsons," a kind of cigarette lighter, because they caught fire easily when hit.

M4 AS APC ▷

Soldiers hitch a ride on an M4 on the island of **Okinawa** in 1945. Many M4s fought against Japanese forces in the Pacific.

Yom Kippur War

In October 1973, Syria and Egypt attacked their neighbor, Israel. The attack took place during the Jewish holiday of Yom Kippur, when most Israeli soldiers were on leave. In the Sinai Desert, Egyptian forces crossed the Suez Canal and broke through the **Bar-Lev** line. On October 14, Egyptian tanks launched their attack. Responding quickly, Israeli armored units surrounded the enemy. The Arab forces were defeated.

AIR AND LAND SUPERIORITY

Israeli M60 advancing, an F4 Phantom overhead. Israel destroyed more than 300 Arab tanks in the Yom Kippur War, losing only 10 of its own.

GOLAN CLASH

Syrian tanks launched a massive attack on the Golan Heights separating Syria and Israel. A small Israeli armored force drove them back. The Israeli 7th Armored Brigade alone destroyed 250 Syrian tanks.

Operation Desert Storm

In 1990 Iraqi leader Saddam Hussein invaded his oil-rich neighbor, Kuwait, in the Middle East. Fearing a similar invasion of Saudi Arabia, the United States and the United Nations (UN) formed a coalition, or group, of nations, to stand against Iraq. Hussein refused to meet a January 17, 1991, deadline to pull out of Kuwait. Coalition forces then launched Operation Desert Storm, an offensive against Iraq. By the end of February, nearly all of Hussein's armored units had been wiped out by ground and air attacks.

IRAQI LOSSES

An Abrams M1 in action in the desert. Iraq lost over 4,000 tanks compared to coalition losses of just 4. Iraq's Soviet-built tanks, airplanes, and tactics proved no match for high-tech weapons like the Abrams tank.

Armor in Afghanistan

ENDURING FREEDOM

Following the September 11, 2001, attacks on the United States, President George W. Bush declared a war on terrorism. The United States and its allies turned their attention to **al-Qaeda** forces in Afghanistan. Al-Qaeda units were equipped with just a few outdated Russian-built tanks. U.S. forces quickly took them out of action.

>> **al-Qaeda** – Islamic terrorist organization led by Osama bin Laden

Enemies of the Tank

Tanks are tough to take out, but they are not unbeatable. Tanks can be blown up by land mines, missiles from the air, by ground-launched rockets, or by other tanks and artillery.

Danger from the Sky

AFVs can be bombed from the air. Aircraft like the A10 Warthog and the Apache helicopter are specially equipped to knock out tanks and mobile artillery. The AH64 Apache was specially designed to hide behind woods or other ground features. It can then pop up and fire its lethal anti-tank missiles before dropping out of sight.

The main anti-armor weapon of the low-and-slow flying A10 is its 30mm high-velocity anti-tank gun. This weapon is a larger version of the standard **gatling gun** fitted to most U.S. combat aircraft. The gatling has an outstanding rate of fire and can shred a tank with 70 armor-piercing shells a second.

Tank-on-tank

Sometimes a tank's worst enemy is another tank. Most modern tanks and anti-tank artillery are equipped with APDS ammunition. This is short for armor-piercing discarding **sabot**. It is a small high-velocity shell that can be fired from a big and powerful gun. Part of the casing falls away, leaving the smaller missile to travel at a higher speed, doing even more damage to the target.

TOW TERROR

Many AFVs and anti-tank aircraft carry TOW—a wire guided anti-tank missile made in the United States. The infantry model is fired from an easy-to-carry stand.

>> **sabot** = a ca

Enemies of the Tank

Stopping 30 tons of heavy metal is a difficult task. It is extremely important, though, if an enemy's armored advance is to be stopped.

BUMPY RIDE

These World War II anti-tank obstacles are still used in modern anti-tank defense. A tracked vehicle can cover most rough ground, but these tall concrete bumps move the tank's tracks.

MINES

Some tanks are fitted with special mine-clearing equipment, like this M72 combat engineer vehicle in Iraq during Operation Desert Storm. The plows in front set off the **mines** before the tracks run over them. Modern anti-tank mines can be difficult to detect, because they are often made of **plastic**.

>> **mine** – an explosive bomb left under the ground that goes off by pressure

ROCKET REVENGE

The RPG-7 handheld anti-tank weapon is made in Russia. It fires a high explosive anti-tank (HEAT) round that can blast through the armor of most tanks. It is fired from the shoulder. The missile has a motor that carries it to the target. A jet of metal and gas blasts a small hole through the armor plate. This sets off the fuel and ammunition inside. The Abrams tank has laminated armor, which is too tough for the RPG-7 to get through.

CONVENTIONAL STEEL ARMOR

Melted metal and gas pierce a hole in ordinary armor.

LAMINATED ARMOR

The HEAT round cannot pierce the Abram's tough armor coating.

STINGER

A U.S. Army instructor teaching a soldier to fire a Stinger anti-tank missile.

Armor around the World

There are many different kinds of AFVs built and operated all over the world. They are expensive to develop, so many countries work together on joint projects. Sales to many different countries helps to pay for development costs.

THE M109

The M109 SPG was introduced in the early 1960s and saw action in Vietnam. It has been continually upgraded since and is still the U.S. Army's main mobile **fire support** weapon.

Details:
Crew: 6
Length: 30 feet
Weight: 27.4 tons
Road Speed: 35 mph
Range: 216 miles
Main Gun: 155mm howitzer
Rate of Fire: 3 rounds/minute
Gun Range: 1 mile

ARIETE MAIN BATTLE TANK

The Ariete is built by Iveco in Italy. The gun ranging system is fully computerized, with laser target finding. It can fire at moving or still targets, even when the tank itself is moving.

Details:
Crew: 4
Length (Hull): 25 feet
Propulsion: Iveco V12 diesel
Road Speed: 40 mph
Main Gun: 120mm **OtoBreda** smoothbore
Capacity: 42 rounds (APDS/HEAT)
Secondary Armament: 2 x 7.62mm machine guns

THE BTR-80

The BTR-80 belongs to Russia's large BMP/BMD armored personnel carrier family. There are many models, including troop transports, rocket launchers, combat patrol, and an SPG. The BTR has seen combat duty in the Middle East and is used by several UN nations.

Details:
Crew: 3, plus 7 troops
Propulsion: 260 hp diesel
Road Speed: 50 mph
Range: 400 miles
Main Armament: 14.5, 7.62mm machine guns
Secondary Armament: 2A72 30mm automatic gun
Rate of Fire: 330 rounds/minute

Armor around the World

MARDER

The Marder armored infantry fighting vehicle was built for the German army. There are many types in service worldwide. Some versions of the Marder are equipped with a **Roland SAM** anti-aircraft missile system and **smoke grenade** launchers.

Details:
Crew: 9
Length: 22 ft. 4 in.
Weight: 28 tons
Road Speed: 46 mph
Range: 325 miles
Main Gun: 20mm cannon
Secondary Armament: 1 x 7.62mm
  machine gun

CHALLENGER 2 MBT

Challenger 2 is the British army's frontline MBT. Manufactured by Vickers, it is equipped with fully computerized laser and infrared target finding, with a powerful smoothbore main gun.

Details:
Crew: 4
Length (Hull): 37 ft.
Weight: 62 tons
Road Speed: 35 mph
Range: 275 miles
Main Gun: 120mm smoothbore
Secondary Armament: 2 x 7.62mm
  machine guns

LAV-25

The LAV-25 is an all-terrain, all-weather vehicle that can operate at night. It can be carried by air and can be made amphibious in just three minutes. It is used by the U.S. Marine Corps.

Details:
Crew: 3, plus 6 troops
Length: 21 ft.
Weight: 12 tons
Road Speed: 62 mph
Main Gun: M242 25mm chain gun 7.62mm machine gun

Armor around the World

PZH 2000

Germany's front-line SPG is the Panzer**haubitze** (PzH) 2000. With a powerful 155mm main gun, it is a full-size, mobile artillery weapon. Developed in 1998, it is in service with several NATO countries.

Details:
Crew: 2
Propulsion: 8-cylinder diesel
Road Range: 260 miles
Main Gun: 155mm L52
Gun Range: 25 miles

XM93 FOX NBC RECONNAISSANCE VEHICLE

The Fox Reconnaissance System is part of the General Dynamics AFV family. The XM93 Fox specializes in **NBC** detection. The crew has a chemical protection system. About 50 Fox vehicles took part in Operation Desert Storm.

Details:
Crew: 4
Length: 22.3 ft.
Weight: 18.7 tons
Road Speed: 65 mph
Road Range: 500 miles
Main Armament: 7.62mm machine gun

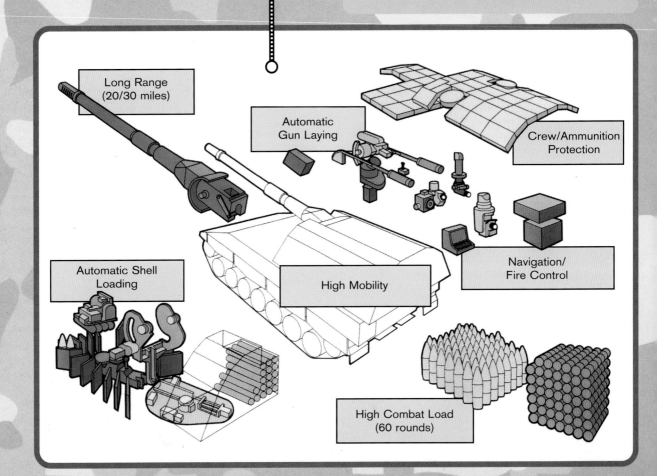

Long Range (20/30 miles)

Automatic Gun Laying

Crew/Ammunition Protection

Automatic Shell Loading

High Mobility

Navigation/ Fire Control

High Combat Load (60 rounds)

M113 APC

An M113 APC. The M113 family of light tracked vehicles is the most widely used AFV in the U.S. forces. There are more than 12 variants, with about 30,000 examples in service.

Details:
Crew: 2, plus 11 troops
Length (hull): 16 ft.
Weight: 12 tons
Road Speed: 41 mph
Range: 300 miles
Main Gun: 0.50 cal. machine gun

T-90

Russia's T-90 is related to the earlier T-72. It is Russia's most advanced MBT, with a new smoothbore main gun and a defensive laser-guided missile system. Both the Russian Federation and the Indian army are equipped with the T-90.

Details:
Crew: 3
Length (hull): 22 ft.
Weight: 44.5 tons
Road Speed: 37 mph
Road Range: 300 miles
Propulsion: multifuel V12
Main Gun: 2A46M smoothbore 125mm, 7.62mm and 12.7mm machine guns
Missiles: Refleks anti-tank guided
Missile Range: 3 miles

CENTAURO

The Centauro reconnaissance anti-tank vehicle is part of a family of **air-portable** wheeled armored cars made by Iveco of Italy. It has a powerful main gun and a light hull. Other variations of the same chassis include an APC and different turret and gun combinations.

Details:
Crew: 4
Length: 27 ft.
Weight: 25 tons
Road Speed: 65 mph
Road Range: 500 miles
Main Gun: 105mm cannon
Secondary Armament: 2 x 7.62mm machine guns

WARRIOR

Warrior is a full NBC-protected, medium AFV used by Great Britain. It is part of a family of vehicles that includes a **Milan** anti-tank missile carrier and a mechanized recovery model.

Details:
Crew: 3
Length: 20 ft.
Weight: 25 tons
Road Speed: 50 mph
Road Range: 400 miles
Main Gun: 30mm Rarden cannon
Secondary Armament: 7.62mm Hughes chain gun

lan = anti

Future Tank Technology

Plans for the next generation of AFVs are already under way. They will have better **stealth technology**, improved defenses, and more firepower. They will also be able to fulfill a variety of combat roles.

NEW ABRAMS

The Abrams M1A2 System Enhancement Program (SEP) will be the front-line MBT for the next decade. It will have high-tech **digital battlefield graphics** and communications equipment.

Future Combat System

The Future Combat System (FCS) is a program of integrated technology for the twenty-first century. The heart of the system, in which different types of equipment work together, is a combination of manned combat vehicles, with smaller robot sensor equipment. Apart from the 40-ton new generation M1A2 Abrams, the systems will be made up of lightweight vehicles. Weighing under 20 tons each, they will be easy to transport by air. The Command and Control (C2) vehicle may be the only manned vehicle within a FCS combat unit. The new Abrams will have state-of-the-art auto-loading and will be about five times more accurate than the M1A1.

ROBOT WARRIORS

The FCS will rely on a coordinated range of radio-controlled, unmanned air and ground vehicles.

Future Combat System (FCS)

Tactical UAV

Control vehicle

Unmanned shooter platform

Robot seeker

Robot sensor

Future Tank Technology

HELLFIRE 2

A new ground-launched version of the Hellfire anti-tank missile is available for some U.S. Army vehicles. The new Hellfire 2 does the same job as TOW but is faster, more powerful, and goes farther. Hellfire proved very effective in the 1991 Gulf War, when fired from Apache helicopters.

WHEELS OR TRACKS

A major concern for many armored vehicle manufacturers is whether to use wheels or tracks. Tracks are heavy, expensive, and difficult to repair but work better on rough terrain. However, **suspension** technology has improved greatly in recent years. The same is true of **differential** axles. Many forces are choosing all-terrain wheeled vehicles. They are lightweight and easier to transport by air. One design for a future combat tank combines road wheels and tracks with an unmanned weapon and a multibarreled cannon.

TRACKS ARE SLOWER THAN WHEELS

Expensive tank transporters are still used to get tanks to the front line. Wheeled vehicles are quicker on paved roads. They can also be quickly put in place by air.

PIRANHA

Switzerland's Piranha armored vehicle is specially designed to cope with the country's mountainous terrain. It is also in use by U.S. Army units.

Special Task Vehicles

Not all future AFVs will have multirole capabilities. This Future Beach Recovery Vehicle is based on the German Leopard chassis. It is specially developed to provide rescue and repair services to amphibious tanks. It will also offer armored protection to rescue teams under fire.

>> **differential** – wheels on independent axles that hold the ground better

Hardware at a Glance

AA = anti-aircraft

AAAV = advanced amphibious assault vehicle

AFV = armored fighting vehicle

APC = armored personnel carrier

APDS = Armor-Piercing Discarding Sabot

ARV = armored reconnaissance vehicle

FCS = Future Combat System

HEAT = High Explosive Anti-Tank

LAV = light armored vehicle

MBT = main battle tank

MLRS = Multiple Launch Rocket System

NATO = North Atlantic Treaty Organization

NBC = nuclear, biological, chemical

SEP = System Enhancement Program

SPG = self-propelled gun

UAV = unmanned aerial vehicle

UN = United Nations

Further Reading & Websites

Ambrose, Stephen E. *The Good Fight: How World War II Was Won.* New York: Atheneum, 2001.

Chasemore, Richard. *Look Inside Cross-Sections: Tanks.* New York: DK Publishing, 1996.

Crismon, Fred W. *U.S. Military Tracked Vehicles.* Osceola, WI: Motorbooks International, 1992.

Dunstan, Simon. *Modern Tanks and AFVs (Vital Guide).* Shrewsbury, UK: Airlife Publishing, 2002.

English, June A. *Scholastic Encyclopedia of the United States at War.* New York: Scholastic, 1998.

Foss, Christopher F. *Jane's Tank & Combat Vehicle Recognition Guide.* New York: Harper Resource, 2000.

Halberstadt, Hans. *Inside the Great Tanks.* Marlborough, UK: Crowood Press, 1998.

Hunicutt, R. P. *Armored Car: A History of American Wheeled Combat Vehicles.* New York: Presidio Press, 2002

Louis, Nancy. *United We Stand: The War on Terrorism.* Edina, MN: Abdo & Daughters, 2002.

Morse, Jennifer Corr. *Military Vehicles (Speed).* San Diego, CA: Blackbirch Marketing, 2001.

Paine, Shepherd. *Modeling Tanks and Military Vehicles.* Brookfield, WI: Kalmbach Publishing, 1982.

Russell, Alan K. *Modern Battle Tanks and Support Vehicles.* Mechanicsburg, PA: Stackpole Books,1997.

Army Technology <http://www.army-technology.com>

DefenseLink <http://www.defenselink.mil>

Federation of American Scientists <http://www.fas.org/man.index.htm/>

Military History Online <http://www.militaryhistoryonline.com>

Military Vehicle Technology Foundation: <http://president@milvehtechfound.com>

NATO multimedia <http://www.nato.int>

Royal Canadian Armoured Corps School <http://www.army.dnd.ca>

U.S. Marine Corps <http://www.usmc.mil>

Places to Visit

You can see examples of some of the tanks and armored fighting vehicles contained in this book by visiting the military museums listed here.

Allegheny Arms and Armor Museum, Smethport, PA <www.armormuseum.com>
American Armored Foundation Tank and Ordnance War Memorial Museum, Danville, VA
American Society of Military History Inter-Service Military Museum, South El Monte, CA
   <http://hometown.aol.com/tankland/museum.htm>
Canadian War Museum, Ottawa, Ontario, Canada <www.civilization.ca/cwm/cwme.asp>
1st Cavalry Division Museum, Ft. Hood, TX <http://pao.hood.army.mil/1cd_museum>
Kenosha Military Museum, Pleasant Prairie, WI <www.kenoshamilitarymuseum.com>
Military Museum of Southern New England, Danbury, CT <www.usmilitarymuseum.org>
Oshawa Military and Industrial Museum, Oshawa, Ontario, Canada <www.ontrmuseum.org>
Patton Museum of Cavalry and Armor, Ft. Knox, KY <http://knox-www.army.mil/museum/>
U.S. Army Ordnance Museum, Aberdeen Proving Ground, MD <www.ordmusfound.org>
Virginia War Museum, Newport News, VA <www.warmuseum.org>
World War II Vehicle Museum and Learning Center, Hubbard, OH
   <www.wwiivehiclemuseum.com>

Index

Picture Sources

Autowrite; 43
British Army Picture Library; 36, 41 (t)
Brown Reference Group; 4, 13, 14, 19, 33 (t, c)
Defense Visual Information Center: 4, 8, 9, 10, 12, 15 (t), 18, 19 (b), 20, 21 (b), 27 (b), 29, 30, 31 (t), 33 (b), 34, 35, 37 (b), 39, 41, 42, 44
General Dynamics; 10 (b), 12, 16–17
Iveco; 40
John Batchelor; 24–25

Krauss-Maffei; 38
M K Dartford; 7 (t), 22, 24–25, 27 (t)
Mowag; 45
Robert Hunt Library; 5, 6, 7 (b), 15 (b), 17, 19 (t), 21 (t), 23, 25, 28, 32
U.S. Army; 14 (t), 18, 31 (b)
ViewTech; 16

3 1524 00544 9501